Kerb

Michael So

T0276658

methuen | drama

LONDON • NEW YORK • OXFORD • NEW DELHI • SYDNEY

METHUEN DRAMA
Bloomsbury Publishing Plc
50 Bedford Square, London, WC1B 3DP, UK
1385 Broadway, New York, NY 10018, USA
29 Earlsfort Terrace, Dublin 2, Ireland

BLOOMSBURY, METHUEN DRAMA and the Methuen
Drama logo are trademarks of Bloomsbury Publishing Plc

First published in Great Britain 2022

Cover Design: Dragonfly Design

Cover Image: Alison Baskerville

A catalogue record for this book is available from the British Library.

A catalog record for this book is available from the Library of Congress.

ISBN: PB: 978-1-3503-3897-5
ePDF: 978-1-3503-3898-2
eBook: 978-1-3503-3899-9

Series: Modern Plays

Typeset by Mark Heslington Ltd, Scarborough, North Yorkshire

To find out more about our authors and books visit
www.bloomsbury.com and sign up for our newsletters.

KERBS

By Michael Southan

Belgrade Theatre, Coventry
Saturday 26 February–Saturday 5 March 2022

Unity Theatre, Liverpool
Wednesday 9 March–Saturday 12 March 2022

Cast, Doncaster
Wednesday 16 March–Friday 18 March 2022

Stephen Joseph Theatre, Scarborough
Wednesday 23 March–Saturday 26 March 2022

Theatre Royal Plymouth
Wednesday 30 March–Saturday 2 April 2022

Cast

Lucy	Maya Coates
David	Jack Hunter
Carol/Toni	Rekha John-Cheriyan

Creative Team

Writer	Michael Southan
Director	Nickie Miles-Wildin
Assistant Director	Britny Virginia
Designer	Amanda Mascarenhas
Lighting and AV Designer	Joshua Pharo
Sound Designer	Charlotte Barber
Movement & Intimacy Director	Angela Gasparetto
Dramaturg	Ola Animashawun
Wordsmith	Kim Hackleman
Audio Description Consultant	Chloë Clarke
Casting Director	Sarah Hughes

Production Team

Production Manager	Callum Finn
Company Stage Manager	Ella Stewart
Relighter	Glyn Edwards
Producers for Graeae	Hetty Shand & Robyn Bowyer
Producer for Belgrade Theatre	Sâmir Bhamra
Film maker	Øyvind Aamli

Access Team

Access Support Workers	Anders Morris Knight, Ashley Hayward, Isabelle Abdul-Rahim, Samuel Normington

With thanks to

The Bearded Butler for the *Kerbs* set build

Kerbs has been made possible with generous funding from Arts Council England, Garfield Weston Foundation and Esmée Fairbairn Foundation.

Maya Coates – Lucy

Maya has trained with numerous theatre organisations including the National Youth Theatre, the Royal Conservatoire of Scotland Junior Theatre Company and Scottish Youth Theatre. She has always had a drive and extreme passion for performing from a young age. She is invested and determined to make the industry more inclusive and pave the way for future disabled artists and theatre makers. Maya completed an HNC diploma in Acting and Performance at the MGA Academy in Edinburgh in 2019. This is Maya's professional stage debut.

Film/TV credits: *McDonald & Dodds* Season 2 (Mammoth Screens for ITV); *Get Even* Season 2 (BBC Netflix); *OUP Kickstart* (Makematic for Oxford University Press).

Radio credit: *Oak Tree Close* (BBC Radio Drama)

As well as acting Maya sat on the Whizz Kidz young board of trustees representing Scotland between 2013 and 2016. In 2017 she took part in photographer Sophie Mayanne's body positivity campaign 'Behind the Scars' which promoted scar awareness.

Jack Hunter – David

Jack graduated with a BA (Hons) in Drama and Performance from Queen Margaret University in 2017.

Theatre credits include: *Cost of Living* (Hampstead Theatre); *Teenage Dick* (Donmar Warehouse); *Romeo and Juliet* (Cumbernauld Theatre); *Swimming for Beginners* (Graeae Theatre Company/British Council/Owlspot Theatre (Tokyo); *All You Need Is LSD* (Told by an Idiot/Birmingham Rep); *Let Me Play the Lion Too* (Told by an Idiot/ Barbican Centre).

TV credits include: *Annika* (Black Camel Pictures); *Traces* (Red Productions).

Radio credits include: *Bartholomew Abominations* (Naked Productions/Graeae Theatre/BBC Radio 4); *Jammed* (EH-FM/Birds of Paradise Theatre).

Jack has also performed his own comedic and poetical works at the Edinburgh Fringe Festival and on the BBC Social.

Rekha John-Cheriyan – Carol/Toni

Rekha is an actor and writer.

In 2021, she was busy filming for Channel 4 and a new film for Working Title as well as returning to the *Trying* cast on Apple TV – all to be released in 2022. She continues to work on a number of corporate projects and runs acting workshops online and in person. Meanwhile, she can be seen in the films *Dream Horse* and *Tomb Raider* and is a recurring member of the cast of Channel 4's *Hollyoaks* as Sheeba.

Michael Southan – Writer

Michael is a playwright and poet from Wolverhampton in the West Midlands. He is an alumnus of Graeae Theatre Company's Write to Play programme (a development programme for deaf and disabled artists) and Birmingham Rep's Foundry scheme. In 2018 he was accepted onto BBC Writersroom's inaugural Writers' Access Group. Michael's radio play *A Moment's Paws* was part of the *Connections* series, nominated for a BBC Audio Drama Award in 2021. His debut poetry pamphlet was published in 2020 by West Midlands spoken word collective *Poets, Prattlers, and Pandemonialists*.

Away from writing, Michael lives with his family and Golden Retriever, Harley. He follows the trials and tribulations of Wolverhampton Wanderers Football Club.

Nickie Miles-Wildin – Director

Nickie is joint Artistic Director and CEO at DaDa. She was previously Associate Director at Graeae Theatre Company where she was head of new writing, and has also worked at Royal Exchange Theatre as Young Company Programme Leader and Resident Assistant Director, part of the Regional Theatre Young Directors Scheme.

Theatre directing credits include: *When This Is Over, Cuttin' It, The Tempest* (Abraham Moss School/Royal Exchange Theatre); *Signal Fires: Beyond Chinatown* (New Earth Theatre); *Crips with Chips, The Iron Man* Library Tour (Graeae/Spark Arts); Rift New Writing Festival (Leeds University/West Yorkshire Playhouse), *The Forest of Forgotten Discos* (Contact /Jackie Hagan); *Buck a Brenda*

& *Bingo Lingo* (co-director/Wild N Beets); *Disability Sex Archives*, *Two Can Toucan* (TwoCan Theatre).

Online work includes: *Crips without Constraints Parts 1 & 2* (Graeae); *Virtual Forest of Forgotten Discos* (Contact); *MMXX* and *ConnectFest* (Royal Exchange Theatre); *Isolation Bingo* (Wild N Beets/First Art).

Audio work includes: *Ghost Pine* by Eve Leigh for Audible, *The Night of the Living Flatpacks* (Naked Productions and Graeae).

Nickie has been Assistant Director at Royal Exchange Theatre, National Theatre, Graeae Theatre Company and Kazzum, as well as Associate Director on *Tommy* (Ramps on the Moon).

In 2014 Nickie co-founded TwoCan, Gloucestershire's first disabled-led theatre company.

Britny Virginia – Assistant Director

Britny is a young emerging director/producer of film, playwright, poet and self-published author. She was born in the beautiful island of St Lucia and much of her work is influenced by her heritage, her disability and her faith.

She has produced/directed several video productions with a poetic narrative, one of which was screened at Channel 4 headquarters and Hoxton Arches after being commissioned by 4Talent on a Content Production programme. She has directed a short monologue piece as part of the 7 Black Woman collective and she has written two plays exploring racial tensions and hair. She has most notably produced, devised and platformed creative events for Theatre Peckham as part of their Spring 2021 resident company NO TABLE. Britny was longlisted for Mad Monologues by Nouveau Riche in 2019 where she explored the trauma of sexual assault. In 2020, she released her first poetry book titled, *So, I'll Stay, Sitting with You*. In 2021 she was shortlisted for two major film competitions, Daniel Alexander Films and Shoot the Company, for her script about disability and romance.

Britny hopes to inspire others, one story at a time!

Amanda Mascarenhas – Designer

Amanda is a theatre designer and visual artist. She works in theatre, television and events. She is also a facilitator, maker and community artist. She is Associate Artist to Kazzum Arts and the King's Head Theatre, and a Trustee of the King's Head Theatre. She graduated from Rose Bruford College of Theatre and Performance gaining BA (Hons) in Theatre Design.

Theatre credits include: *The Sorcerers Apprentice* (Northern Stage); *Coming Clean* (Trafalgar Studios); *Cuttin' It* (Royal Exchange Theatre); *Everything Has Changed* (New Diorama Theatre); *Our Voice, Our Way* (Wellcome Trust); *Wonder Girl* (Ovalhouse); *Anna Hibiscus* (Discovery Centre); *Tilbury Carnival* (Royal Opera House); *Mole and Gecko* (RUA Arts tour); *La Traviata* (Kings Head Theatre); *Run it Back* (Talawa Theatre); *Much Ado About Nothing* (Merely Theatre EU tour); *A Sublime Feeling* (Salisbury Playhouse); 'Big 30' exhibition (Southbank Centre); *The Boy and the Mermaid* (Paper Balloon); *East Meets West* (Soho Theatre); *Scrub a Dub* (Half Moon Theatre).

Website: www.amandamascarenhas.com

Twitter: @AmandaM_Design

Instagram: @amanda.m_design

Joshua Pharo – Lighting and AV Designer

Joshua works as a lighting and projection designer across theatre, dance, opera, music, film and art installation.

Theatre credits include: *Jekyll & Hyde* (National Theatre); *Wolf Witch Giant Fairy* (Royal Opera House); *Love and Other Acts of Violence* (Donmar Warehouse); *Extinct* (Theatre Royal Stratford East); *The Litten Trees* (Fuel Theatre); *Crave* (Chichester Festival Theatre); *The Bee in Me* (Unicorn Theatre); *Cinderella* (Lyric Hammersmith); *Vassa* (Almeida Theatre); *Noughts & Crosses* (UK tour); *Going Through* (Bush Theatre); *Future Bodies* (HOME); *Nanjing* (Sam Wanamaker Playhouse); Medea (Gate Theatre); *Removal Men* (Yard Theatre); *La Tragédie de Carmen* (Royal Opera House/Wilton's Music Hall); *Cosmic Scallies* (Royal Exchange Theatre/Graeae); *Burning Doors* (Belarus Free Theatre); *Bodies* (Royal Court); *How My Light Is Spent* (Royal Exchange Theatre);

Scarlett (Hampstead Theatre/Theatr Clwyd); *The Twits* (Curve Theatre); *Contractions* (Crucible Theatre); *Julie* (Northern Stage); *We're Stuck!* (China Plate); *The Bear/The Proposal* (Young Vic).

TV/film credit: *Where I Go (When I Can't Be Where I Am)* for Rachel Bagshaw & China Plate.

Charlotte Barber – Sound Designer

Charlotte goes by the moniker SHAR and is a sound designer, multimedia performer and artist. She writes and produces music for theatre, film and live performance.

Credits include: *Still Breathing* (Manchester International Festival); *Utopia* (Royal Exchange Theatre); *Up the Hill* (Royal Exchange Theatre); *Belle and Mary* (The Dukes); *the accident did not take place* (YESYESNONO); *Insert Slogan Here* (YESYESNONO).

Angela Gasparetto – Movement and Intimacy Director

Credits include: *Girl on the Train* (The English Theatre, Frankfurt); *The Long Song* (Chichester Festival Theatre); *Earthquakes* (Guildhall School of Music & Drama); *The Tyler Sisters* (Hampstead Theatre); *One Under* (UK tour Graeae & Theatre Royal Plymouth); *Macbeth* (Chichester Festival Theatre); *Blood Knot* (Orange Tree Theatre); *Eden* (Hampstead Theatre); *Blasted* (RADA); *Home Sweet Home* (Stratford Circus & tour); *The Tempest* (Royal Exchange Theatre); *Frankenstein* (Royal Exchange Theatre); *It Is So Ordered* (Pleasance Theatre); *Wish List* (Royal Exchange Theatre & Royal Court Theatre); *Snowflakes* (Oxford Playhouse); *Juliet* (BBC4/Barbican Centre); *Sizwe Banzi Is Dead* (Young Vic); *A Midsummer Night's Dream* Custom/Practice Theatre (Almeida Festival & Edinburgh Fringe).

Ola Animashawun – Dramaturg

Ola is a National Theatre Associate and Connections Dramaturg and the co-founder and Creative Director of the playwriting consultancy Euphoric Ink. He is also a former Associate Director of the Royal Court Theatre, where he worked for twenty-three years, during which time he founded and ran the Royal Court Young

Writers' Programme, and set up a nationwide writers' programme – Critical Mass – which is dedicated to finding and nurturing new playwrights from the Global Majority.

Ola has worked in theatre for over thirty years, with twenty of those years dedicated to specialising in script development as a dramaturg and facilitator. He has also held positions as an Associate Artist, Dramaturg and Mentor for Belgrade Theatre, Everyman Theatre, Theatre Absolute, Shop Front Theatre and Eclipse Theatre.

His other skills include acting, directing, devising, writing and presenting.

He is a patron of Graeae Theatre and Script Yorkshire and an Honorary Fellow of the Royal Central School of Speech and Drama. He is also an Alfred Fagon Black Champion of Theatre.

Kim Hackleman – Wordsmith

Kim Hackleman is a writer, director, actor, producer and poet. She has written plays, short stories and co-written a musical. Her poem, 'Weaving Coventry', was commissioned by Coventry City Council and features as part of the water rills which run through a newly refurbished area of the city centre. The rills are small decorative channels carrying water and the words of her poem, which have been carved out of granite, are situated inside of these rills. Her piece 'The Birthday Gift' was commissioned by the Royal Shakespeare Company and Coventry City of Culture 2021 as part of the City Voices programme for *Faith*. Her poem 'I Too Am an Immigrant' has just been published in the poetry anthology, *Poetry and Settled Status for All*. *Kerbs* is her first credit as 'Wordsmith'. She is from the USA and now lives in Coventry, England with her husband, two sons and dog.

Chloë Clarke – Audio Description Consultant

Chloë Clarke began her career as an Audio Description Consultant in 2014 following the success of her own project exploring creative, integrated AD that offers a choice of interpretation to the visually impaired audience and eliminates the need for headsets.

Since then she has worked steadily for a large variety of venues and companies to facilitate the integration of creative AD into their work, some of which include Graeae, Leeds Playhouse, Theatre Royal Plymouth, Liverpool Everyman & Playhouse, Manchester Royal Exchange, Wales Millennium Centre and Warner Bros. Entertainment.

Sarah Hughes – Casting Director

Sarah Hughes is Alan Ayckbourn's casting director and has also freelanced extensively for the Entertainment Department of the BBC and in TV comedy. Other theatre work includes plays for Leeds Playhouse, Theatre By The Lake, Birmingham Rep, Stafford Shakespeare Festival, Out of Joint, Northern Broadsides, Theatre Royal Northampton and many projects with Graeae, Access All Areas and for Frantic Assembly. She was a Senior Cast Co-Ordinator for the London 2012 opening and closing ceremonies and is often involved with casting large outdoor site-specific projects such as the Greenwich and Docklands Festival. She has worked for the Stephen Joseph Theatre in Scarborough for a number of years as the SJT's casting director. She is a member of the Casting Directors' Guild, and also works as a teacher and lecturer.

CELEBRATING *FOUR* DECADES

Recently celebrating its fortieth anniversary in 2021, **Graeae** is an acclaimed and award-winning theatre company, existing to cultivate and champion the best in Deaf and disabled talent on the UK and international stages.

Recent productions and co-productions have included *10 Nights*, two seasons of the digital new work programme *Crips without Constraints*, *Signal Fires*, *One Under*, the hit Ian Dury musical *Reasons to Be Cheerful*, *The House of Bernarda Alba* starring Kathryn Hunter, *Blood Wedding*, *The Threepenny Opera*, and outdoor epics *The Iron Man* and *This Is Not for You*. In 2022, they will stage their first opera, *The Paradis Files*, a newly commissioned piece by renowned composer Errollyn Wallen OBE.

With Naked Productions for BBC Radio 4, Graeae have also produced radical reinterpretations of classic drama in recent years, including *Bartholomew Abominations*, *Three Sisters*, *Amy Dorrit* and *Midwich Cuckoos*.

In addition to productions, Graeae also runs an extensive programme of training, learning and creative professional development programmes throughout the year including Ensemble for young theatre-makers and the Beyond scheme, to help Deaf and disabled artists to flourish and grow.

Since 1997, Graeae has been run by Jenny Sealey MBE, who also co-directed the London 2012 Paralympic Opening Ceremony.

Artistic Director and Joint CEO: Jenny Sealey MBE

Executive Director and Joint CEO: Kevin Walsh

Finance Director: Charles Mills

Board of trustees: Samantha Tatlow (Chair), Caroline Jane Loving, Sharon Marshall, Lisa A. Oguntoyinbo, Jessi Parrott, Tim Powell, Nathan Crossan-Smith, Anthony Lee.

Patrons: Jenny Agutter OBE, Ola Animashawun, Sir Peter Blake CBE, Matt Bray, Hilary Carty OBE, Jemima Dury, Mat Fraser, Sadie Frost, Ruth Fabby MBE DL, Nabil Shaban, Jack Thorne, Emma Thompson DBE, Dame Harriet Walter DBE, Richard Wilson OBE.

www.graeae.org

Twitter: @graeae

Facebook: @graeae

Instagram: @graeaetheatrecompany

Graeae are a registered charity (no. 284589), and can be supported by visiting justgiving.com/Graeae.

Supported using public funding by
ARTS COUNCIL ENGLAND
LOTTERY FUNDED

The Belgrade Theatre was built in 1958 as part of the reconstruction of Coventry after World War II. Holding 858 in its two-tier main auditorium, and 250–300 in the flexible, second space, B2, it remains one of the largest regional producing theatres in Britain.

Autumn 2007 saw the re-opening of the Belgrade Theatre after completion of its £14 million redevelopment project, including the creation of B2, and refurbishment of the existing listed building.

Having started the Theatre-in-Education (TIE) movement in the 1960s, the Belgrade also continues to pioneer new initiatives in this field as well as other community and outreach programmes.

A key partner of Coventry UK City of Culture 2021, the Belgrade Theatre's 2021 programme has been led by three artists from diverse backgrounds, under the role of Co-Artistic Directors, alongside members of the local community. Corey Campbell, Balisha Karra and Justine Themen are developing a new vision and way of working for a twenty-first century theatre, bringing with them a unique perspective that celebrates Coventry's diversity and drives positive change. The KEYS project aims to achieve a strategic shift to embed diversity, community collaboration and talent development at the heart of the theatre process.

As of January 2022, the Belgrade are proud to have Laura Elliot as their new CEO and Corey Campbell as their Creative Director.

Forthcoming productions include: *Fighting Irish*, *Nothello*, *May Queen* and the innovative digital project *SeaView*.

CEO: Laura Elliot

Creative Director: Corey Campbell

Board of trustees: David Hanson (Chair), Alan Pollock (Vice Chair), Cllr Roger Bailey, Shelia Bates, Colin Bell, Paul Carvell, Nyasha Daley, Annette Hay, Tyrone Huggins, Thanh Sinden, Tony Skipper, Rebecca Warwick and Jon Wilby

www.belgrade.co.uk

Twitter: @BelgradeTheatre

Facebook: @BelgradeTheatreCoventry

Instagram: @belgradetheatre

TikTok: @belgradetheatre

As a registered charity (number 219163), the Belgrade creates and uses the transformational power of theatre to enrich communities and change people's lives for the better.

Coventry UK City of Culture 2021 commenced on 15 May 2021, running for 12 months. The 365-day cultural programme reflects Coventry as a diverse, modern city, demonstrating that culture is a force that changes lives. Coventry is the UK's only city of peace and reconciliation, and known internationally as a city of welcome, a city of activists and pioneers, innovation and invention, and now a City of Culture.

Coventry is the city where movement began; from innovation in the transport industry to a history of welcome, it has moved people for centuries. For a whole year, Coventry is celebrating with events, music, dance, theatre and large-scale spectacle. As well as the expected celebrations, it is throwing a spotlight onto city voices with a range of hyper local experiences and ways to get involved across every neighbourhood. And it's not just Coventry. This epic celebration also sees the entire region getting involved and benefitting from the opportunities that being City of Culture brings.

The year of culture is co-created with the people of Coventry and is bringing about long-term social, economic and cultural benefits.

Coventry City of Culture Trust is grateful for the support of the following partners:

Principal Partners
Coventry City Council, West Midlands Combined Authority, Department for Digital, Culture, Media & Sport, Arts Council England, The National Lottery Heritage Fund, The National Lottery Community Fund, Spirit of 2012, Warwickshire County Council, University of Warwick, Coventry University

Major Partners
Coventry Building Society, Paul Hamlyn Foundation

International Partner
British Council

Honorary Partner
Positive Youth Foundation

Regional Partner
Coventry Building Society Arena

Transport Partners
Avanti West Coast, National Express Coventry

City Champions
Backstage Trust, Coventry College, Esmée Fairbairn Foundation, Exasoft Group, Foyle Foundation, Garfield Weston Foundation, Orbit Group, Patrick Trust, PET-Xi, Severn Trent

Other Partners
Art Fund, Cadent Foundation, Jerwood Arts, Saintbury Trust, The Eveson Charitable Trust, The Linbury Trust, The Radcliffe Trust

Delivery Partners
Coventry Business Improvement District, Coventry & Warwickshire Chamber of Commerce, Coventry & Warwickshire Local Enterprise Partnership, EnV, Heart of England Community Foundation, West Midlands Police

Acknowledgements

Tim, Karen, Chloe and Molly Southan for always believing in me and enduring endless traffic jams and train journeys. Everyone at Graeae for commissioning the play. Nickie Miles-Wildin for her patience, generosity and creative vision that brought *Kerbs* to life. Ola Animashawun for helping me to shape the world of the play. Tom Wells, for being the best mentor ever and believing in the play early on. Tessa Walker for the weekly phone calls. Write To Play Year 4: Khush Chahal, Karran Collings, Jessica Lovett, Hannah Torrence and Naomi Westerman for the biscuit chat and nights out in the chain pubs of Wolverhampton. Hayley Rogers for her friendship, support and twelve-year long Messenger chat.

Michael Southan

Kerbs

Characters

David
Lucy
Carol
Toni

Social Media Key:

____ emoji* = when we see an emoji projected

 # = when we see a hashtag projected

Hashtag = when someone says 'Hashtag'

Prologue

Projection montage.

Lucy *on non-disabled dating app – show her being ghosted or trolled/fetishised.*

Lucy *on disabled dating app.*

Lucy *matches with* **David**.

David   *'Hey match.'*

Lucy   *'One night stand?'*

David   *'Good start.'*

Lucy   *'Or one night sit . . . on your lap . . . *crying laughing face emoji*'*

David   *'You have my full attention.'*

Lucy   *'What are you in the mood for?'*

David   *'Drinks? *wine emoji*'*

Lucy   *'Cock-tails. *aubergine emoji* LOL'*

David   *'*laughing crying face emoji*'*

Lucy   *'*cocktail emoji*'*

David   *'I know just the place.'*

Lucy   *'My housemate is out till 9.30.'*

David   *'6.30 p.m. drinks first? A little lubrication?'*

Lucy   *'Purr-fect. Then back to mine for a quickie in the quickie'*

David   *'You. Are. On!'*

Scene One

Date – Friday night

It is Friday night, 8 p.m. The light from a street lamp shines down on stage. **Lucy** *enters the stage like a firework, driving a powered wheelchair.*

Lucy (*entering*)   Yes, my man, work those wheels. And that is the wrist action of a true pro.

David   I'm just warming up.

She turns to face him as he enters the stage.

Lucy   Well, don't hold back. Share the love. I'm freezing my tits off out here.

David   So I see.

Lucy   Cheeky fuck.

David   Precisely. Maybe two – if your housemate sticks to their promise and stays out as long as you say they will.

Lucy   Brave talk, from someone who's been on a 'break' while they concentrate on their studies.

David   Been saving it up for the right person. I don't just talk the talk, I roll the hole.

Lucy   Is that so?

David   Never had any complaints. I only do moans of mutual appreciation. And there's been plenty of those.

Lucy   Are you for real?

David   I am.

Lucy   But what if you're a bit rusty?

David   Like all good wheelies, I've got oil in my bag . . .

Lucy   Oh yeah . . . shall I rub it on your joystick?

David   Well, if it's a smooth ride you're after . . .

Lucy   Not too smooth . . . (**Lucy**'s *alarm on her phone goes.*) Come on, we've got to get back and make some noise!

David   Yes.

Lucy   Yes.

David   Yes!

Lucy   Yes!

David   Yes!

Lucy   Oh yes!

David   Ohhh, your wheels are on fire!

Lucy   Hashtag wheels on fire!

Simultaneously, **Lucy** *sets off at speed but suddenly hits the kerb, knocking her out of her chair.* **David** *is oblivious.*

Lucy   FUUUUUCCCCKKKKK! Ow! Fuck! Fuck, fuck, fuck.

She tries to get up but can't . . .

Fuck, fuck, fuck.

David *turns and sees* **Lucy** *on the pavement and realises what has happened. He takes out the earphones and wheels back to her.*

David   Lucy! Are you okay?

Lucy   No! It hurts like fuck!

David   Shit!

Lucy   David, call my mum.

David   Yeah, okay, um . . .

Lucy   Get my phone.

David   Okay . . . um . . .

Lucy   Fucking hell!

David *bends down with the phone to get* **Lucy**'s *eyes – it opens.*

David   Shiiit. Right, what's your mum's name?

Lucy   It's under mum.

David   Yes, course.

Lucy   Put it on speaker phone and go.

David   What?

Lucy   Just go David. Go!

David   I'm not leaving you on your own.

Lucy   I won't be on my own. My mum will be here soon. She doesn't live too far away.

David   But what /

Lucy   David. Go. Please. It's easier this way.

Pause.

David *presses the phone and hands it to* **Lucy***.*

Phone is ringing.

Lucy   Thank you.

David   No . . . problem . . .

Phone is ringing. **David** *goes to leave. We hear* **Carol** *say 'Lucy' and* **Lucy** *urgently and silently motions for* **David** *to go with her good arm as lights fade . . .*

Scene Two

Hospital One – Saturday morning

Lucy *in bed lying motionless.* **Carol** *by the side. We hear the closing bars of a well-known song, a song that* **Carol** *thinks* **Lucy** *loves, being played on* **Carol***'s phone. When it finishes* **Carol** *stares at* **Lucy** *hard – looking for signs of life – and then waves her hand in front of* **Lucy***'s face. No response from* **Lucy***.*

Carol   Oh, Lucy, love.

Slight pause.

I know, what about this? You love this one.

Carol *starts playing 'Dancing Queen' on her phone.* **Lucy** *wakes up with a start, tries to hold her head with her injured hand, revealing her wrist in a cast.*

Lucy (*referring to her head – she has a raging headache from her hangover and her fall – and then referring to her wrist*)   Ow! Ow! Fucksake, Mum, what are you doing, turn it off!

Carol (*turning the music off*)   Darling, you're awake. Thank the Lord.

Lucy   'Course I'm awake, the whole ward's probably awake now. What's with the mobile disco?

Carol   I was worried, I thought maybe you'd slipped /

Lucy   I did slip, I told you, I hit a kerb.

Carol   No, slipped into a coma overnight, so I was playing you something familiar, something to penetrate your deep state of unconsciousness.

Lucy   I should be so lucky.

Carol   Anyway, looks like it worked didn't it? Thank goodness you're back with us.

Lucy   Mum, I had a local anaesthetic, I was conscious the whole time.

Carol   You can't be too careful. You could've been concussed, had a delayed reaction, become locked in.

Lucy   The only thing locked in is the beating rhythm in my head. Can you just dial it down, by about 1000 decibels please?

Carol   Actually no, Lucy, I can't dial it down /

Lucy   Urgh. (*In a kind of 'give me a break' and 'my head really hurts' kind of way.*)

Carol   Not until I get some answers . . . and an apology.

Lucy   Sorry, Mum.

Carol   I should think so.

Lucy   Now can I have some painkillers?

Carol   Answers first. Lying spreadeagled in the middle of the high street, showing off your assets, could've caused a multiple pile-up if I hadn't got there so quickly.

Lucy   Mum, it was no big deal.

Carol   What on earth happened?

Lucy   I just fell out my chair. Hit the kerb funny.

Carol   Well, I'm not laughing.

Lucy   I went out for some drinks. To have fun. Like people do.

Carol   Ah, it's all coming out now.

Lucy   What is? And what is this, *Line of Duty*?

Carol   Have a few cocktails did you?

Lucy   Maybe. So, it's not a crime.

Carol   No, but the state you got yourself into is criminal.

Lucy   Hashtag accidents happen.

Carol   Exactly, which is why you should not have been alone! Where was Aleesha?

Lucy   Let's just say she was otherwise engaged.

Carol   Right, snogging the face off some joker she'd just met on one of those apps then, no doubt.

Lucy   Amazing, it's like you have three eyes.

Carol   I knew it. She's not had her head screwed on right, ever since she started on these dating apps.

Lucy   I don't think it's Aleesha's head you should be concerning yourself with when it comes to screwing.

Carol   Well, I do. I tell you, Luce, best to steer clear of 'em.

Lucy   I don't know, they don't seem that bad.

Carol   They are. They sidetrack you from the people you love . . . and the people who love you!

Lucy   All right, but don't be so hard on Aleesha, she's only doing what people our age do. And look, I'm ok.

Carol   Yes, but my point is, it could have been so much worse . . . you were alone, vulnerable. Women have to be doubly careful . . . you understand me, Luce?

Lucy   Yes, I understand you, every last syllable, but please, can you get me some painkillers, before I slip into a mother-induced coma.

Carol   Ok, I'll find a nurse, but better still, what about a hot chocolate. Cream? Marshmallows? The works? I think we deserve it! Well, I do, you certainly don't. Don't go wandering off, I will be right back.

Carol *leaves.* **Lucy** *checks her phone. She sees social media of* **Aleesha** *out with several different men at different times.*

There is a knock at the door. **David** *is at the open door. He carries a bag for life.*

David   Emergency care package.

Lucy *is very surprised to see him and embarrassed by being in a hospital gown in bed.*

Lucy   What . . .?

David   I've got magazines and grapes. That's what people usually get isn't it?

Lucy   How . . .?

David   Only one hospital in town and only one sexy young thing in that hospital.

Lucy   David, I think you should leave . . .

David   Don't worry, I am not stalking you, I just wanted to make sure you are ok.

Lucy   Look, I know how to take care of myself.

David   But you had me ring your mum instead of your housemate.

Lucy   So?

David   So that sounds bad!

Lucy   It wasn't bad. I'm ok, will everyone just chill!

David   Well, you could have at least let me wait with you until she arrived! It was like you thought your mother might . . .

Lucy   Kill you? Yes, she might have and she still might if she knew. She has just nipped out and is coming back any minute so . . .

David *wheels into the room and comes up to* **Lucy**.

David   Alright, I just wanted to bring you these. Don't worry, I can't stay. Thesis deadline Monday. I'll pop them down here for you.

He pulls a bunch of flowers out of the bag and places them purposefully on the night table.

Lucy   David, we don't know each other. One swipe right hardly deems it necessary to bring a person flowers in the hospital.

David   Lucy, come on, we had fun last night.

Lucy   Speak for yourself. Please, just go.

He just looks at her.

Look, I'll text you, I'll text you when I'm feeling better.

David Alright.

David *leaves.*

Beat.

Carol *comes in with two paper cups with lids.*

Carol Well, they didn't have marshmallows, they didn't have cream, we're lucky they even had hot chocolate!

She hands one to **Lucy** *and pulls a straw out of nowhere and puts it into the drink.*

Carol Mind yourself. Hot drinks through a straw, not best really, do you remember that one time . . .

Lucy I was five, Mum, five! I am not a kid anymore. I don't still need you buying me hot chocolates and I definitely do not need marshmallows!

Carol Alright, Luce, it is just a hot chocolate! I told you I was going for hot chocolate. You are so changeable. Come on. I know the fall must have scared you . . .

Lucy It did not scare me, Mum, I am fine. I just need them to release me.

Carol Look, love, they said it's happening later today.

Lucy Yes, but when?

Carol It doesn't matter, you just need to relax and let that wrist of yours heal.

Lucy Mum, why don't you go home. I haven't forgotten it's Toni's birthday do in The Blacksmith's Arms tonight. Go home now get a bit of rest and you'll have plenty of energy to dance the night away later on.

Carol No. I need to be here, for you. Toni will be getting enough attention from the rest of her friends, she won't even notice I'm not there. Besides, it won't be all that, everyone sat down, two metres apart, it'll hardly be a rave will it?

Lucy   Actually, I think Toni's needs are greater than mine right now. This will be her first birthday without Christine.

Carol   If you can't go then I'm not going to go and leave you all alone at home. She'll understand.

Lucy   Go celebrate with Toni, Mum, please. You could be waiting for hours for me to get discharged. You know what hospitals are like. Go and enjoy yourself. You both deserve it. Stop worrying about me. I'll be fine.

Carol   But I do worry. It's in my job description.

Lucy   Please, Mum, I'm an adult! I can take care of myself. I am just going to watch Netflix and chill.

Carol   Are you sure?

Lucy   I'll be fine. I'll order an Uber as soon as I get the all-clear.

Carol   Alright, but make sure we get that nice bloke Gary who dropped you off last time. He had a lovely accessible Kangoo, very spacious.

Lucy   Was it just the size of his Kangoo you were interested in?

Carol   Who brought you all of this?

Lucy   Uh, Aleesha stopped by to see how I was. I told you not to be so hard on her.

Carol   So I just missed her?

Lucy   I told her how disappointed in her you are, and she suddenly remembered she had something important to do.

Carol   Like I said. Never the same since the apps.

Lucy   Mum, please just go and have fun. I will be fine.

Carol   Alright, but text me if you need anything.

Lucy   I will. Can you pass me my phone before you go?

Carol   See you do still need me.

She kisses **Lucy** *on the forehead and leaves.*

Lucy *immediately grabs her phone.*

Lucy (*texting* **David**)   *'What are you doing tonight?'*

David   *'Are you feeling better?'*

Lucy   *'Yes. But I could be feeling even better than this.'*

David   *'I think I've got something for that.'*

Lucy   *'I have been very naughty, doctor, you're going to have to examine me . . .'*

David   *'OK.'*

Lucy   *'My housemate's out tonight, let's pick up where we left off.'*

David   *'I'll go grab my stethoscope.'*

Lucy   *'I like a man who cums properly attired.'*

David   *'And I like a patient who knows what's good for them.'*

Lucy   *'Oh yes, doctor, I know. And I'm making myself ready to show you when you get here.'*

Pause.

'Doctor . . .?'

David   *'You've just blown the top off my thermometer.'*

Scene Three

Hospital Two – Saturday evening

Lucy *is sat up in her chair, the bed is made, a holdall of clothes sits on it. Her arm is in a sling, supporting her wrist.* **David** *is at the open door.*

Lucy (*voice of a patient*)   Hello, are you my doctor or my ride?

David   Both. Your carriage awaits.

Lucy   Oh thank you, doctor, but wait, I'm suddenly feeling . . . all of a . . .

David *wheels into the room, closer to her.*

David   Tell me, quickly explain your symptoms, so I can get a better feel for things.

Lucy   I'm just very . . . uptight doctor . . . and hot . . . all of the time.

David   Of course, it's hard to tell without an examination.

Lucy   Indeed. Full body. I think it's rather urgent . . .

David   Well, let's get you home and laid up in bed immediately. There's no time to lose.

Lucy   Take me with your stethoscope doctor, only your expertise can help me now.

They kiss passionately.

Let's go.

David   Absolutely, this is an emergency.

Lucy   I've got Nutella in the fridge.

David   Exactly what I was going to prescribe.

Lucy   Applied liberally.

David   And taken orally.

Lucy   Be prepared to learn a thing or two yourself, doctor.

David   You're good at this.

Lucy   And not only this.

She leaves, **David** *wheels after her. After a while,* **David** *wheels back in and picks up* **Lucy***'s clothes bag and wheels out.*

Scene Four

Party – Saturday night

A dark stage. **Toni** *enters, face lit by the laptop she is carrying. She turns on the lights.*

Carol   Toni, I just had a message from her. She's in the cab. You set up the drinks. I've got to finish the cake.

Toni (*shouting to the other room*)   No problem, Carol. I'm on it. I've got the laptop for Zoom.

She is looking for a place to put the laptop down.

(*Shouting to the other room.*) Carol, come in here, we can set it up in front of the sofa!

Toni *chatting, audio describing who is on the Zoom call while she sets the laptop on the coffee table, sits on the sofa facing it and a Zoom call appears onstage.*

Toni (*talking to the laptop*)   All right, everyone, cameras off now, so there's no inopportune light coming out of the screen. Mute yourselves too for that matter, I know what some of you are like once you get excited, specially you, Colin, you can't contain yourself. What was that? It's not the seal on your lips I'm worried about. Now button it. Remember, when we hear her coming in, I'll hit the lights, you all turn your cameras and mics on and shout 'Surprise!' Carol, come on, or she'll be here. Right, I'm turning these lights out now.

Just as **Toni** *goes to hit the lights* **Lucy** *and* **David** *come flying into the living room, in a state of undress. Everyone on the Zoom call shouts 'SURPRISE!'*

Toni   Shit, Lucy, you're early. Carol is going to be gutted she missed your entrance. Lucy! Welcome home! Say hello to everyone on Zoom!

Everyone on Zoom cheers.

Lucy   Toni! What's going? I thought you were out with Mum, celebrating.

Toni   Well, we obviously weren't just going to leave you to it. Not after your ordeal –

Lucy   It's neither an ordeal nor a big deal, I've just –

Toni   Quiet, you – if the girl can't come to the party – the party will have to come to you –

More cheers from the Zoom call. **Lucy** *waves back awkwardly.*

Toni   So we've mugged off the pub and we're having a Zoom do instead – can't be breaking any government regulations and have a house full can we? I mean who'd do a thing like that? Though I see you've brought in some real life entertainment for yourself.

Lucy   Oh, sorry yeah, this is David . . . David, this is Toni.

David   Um, yeah, I just wanted to make sure she got home ok. You must be Lucy's housemate, I've hea /

Lucy   Well, what a surprise, Toni! Great to see all of you! Hashtag loving my life.

Toni   Is it windy out? You look like you've been dragged through a hedge backwards.

Lucy   Yeah, (*lifting her top back up to her shoulder*) just a bit windy.

Toni   You'll need to get your breath back if you're going to do karaoke.

Lucy   Karaoke? . . .

Toni   Well, there ain't no party like an S Club party, and you've got to have karaoke for that haven't you? Never done it exclusively on Zoom before mind you. Hope there isn't too much delay.

David   Look, er, Lucy I think I'll /

Lucy (*to* **David**)   Just a sec. (*To* **Toni**.) Where's Mum?

Toni   In the kitchen getting all the food ready, you know what she's like. She was having a fight with a genoise, and at last check the genoise was winning. Hey, maybe you two could go out and come back in again, pretend you haven't arrived yet, so she isn't disappointed.

David   Yes, Lucy, we wouldn't want to disappoint your *mum*.

Toni   Do you like karaoke, David?

David   Thanks for the invitation, but it's not quite what I thought was on the menu for tonight.

Toni   You have not lived until you have heard Lucy and Carol do 'Dancing Queen'.

David   I can imagine.

Toni   Now, shug. Now that you're here, let's get this party started! Can I get you both some nibbles?

Lucy   Please, and do you want to take the Zoom party with you, while I hang up our coats. I'll be there in a sec.

Toni   When I come back, David, we're doing a duet – you and me – a bit of Sonny and Cher. (*Singing.*) I got you babe . . . I got you babe . . . Carol!

She disappears.

David   Aw, and I was so looking forward to meeting your housemate when they came home.

Lucy   David, I'm sorry. Mum was meant to be out.

David   That is not the point, Lucy.

Lucy   It's not a big deal.

David   Yeah, you're right, Lucy, it's not a big deal that you live with your mum, but it is a big deal that you lied to me about it.

Lucy   I just thought if I told you . . .

David   What?

Lucy   You'd be all . . .

David   Yes?

Lucy   Like this. Exactly like this.

David   Well, I'm sorry, but when you said you wanted to sit on my lap I didn't think it was to role playing being back in the nursery.

Lucy   What do you mean?

David   I'm glad there's a load of people who really care about you. But I'm not here for a game of happy families.

Lucy   Look, you don't know me. But I thought /

David   No, and you don't know me. This isn't for me.

Lucy   Fine. Ok.

David   When you're ready to handle some real adult fun let me know, eh?

Lucy   David. David!

He rolls out.

Lucy *is left alone on stage and we can hear 'Dancing Queen' starting to play,* **Carol** *starting to sing and it all getting closer and closer.*

Scene Five

Throughout the Week

Lucy *centre stage.* **Carol** *pops out upstage left.*

Carol   Morning darling. How you feeling? How's your wrist?

Lucy   Not great.

Carol   Do you want a cushion to elevate it? Let me get you one.

Lucy   Thanks, Mum.

Carol *downstage left.*

Carol   What have you eaten today? You need to keep your strength up.

Lucy   Toast and eggs.

Carol   Just that on its own / No, that's not enough /

Lucy   / Mum.

Carol   I'll do you sausage and bacon. Fried bread – a mid-week treat.

Lucy   Urgh.

Projection: Snapchat Of Aleesha in Lanzarote with Luke #Lanzahottie.

Carol *downstage right.*

Carol   Good morning, good morning! I've cancelled coffee with Toni. Let's go for a wheel in the park.

Lucy   I've got a headache.

Carol   Fresh air will do you good.

Lucy   Mum. No.

Carol   Are you / sure I can.

Lucy   Mum, please!

Carol   Okay.

Time passes.

Lucy   Get back out there Lucy_BunnyGuurl_2001 . . . Whose out to play tonight? Oh hello, Jakeboy69 . . .

Projection: Lucy on dating app. She swipes right.

Notification of a match.

Jakeyboy69   '*Hi. I'm usually the one who puts women in wheelchairs . . .*'

Lucy   What the actual . . .? Delete.

Lucy *deletes the app.* **Carol** *upstage left.*

Carol   I've got a surprise for us!

Lucy   What now?

Carol   I've booked us onto an online French class. Tomorrow night. On Zoom.

Lucy   What fun for a Friday night!

Carol   *Voulez-vous coucher avec moi . . .*

Lucy   Do you know what that means?

Carol   No, but I soon will!

Scene Six

Talk – Later that night

Lucy *is sat at the sink washing dishes. She is doing it intensely.* **Carol** *enters.*

Carol   Lucy preparing *le fromage*, I've seen it all now. Don't worry, I won't tell the DWP.

Lucy   Hmmm.

She continues.

Carol   Lovely sunset tonight. Always feel a bit lighter when the weather's changing, nature's way of telling you it'll get better.

Lucy   I guess so, yeah.

Carol   Don't you think?

Lucy   Absolutely, yes.

Carol   I'm looking forward to this French class tonight.

Lucy   Mmmm.

Carol   Do you think we'll actually have to chat to everyone in French?

Lucy   Maybe.

Carol   You going to join on your phone or shall we both be on the laptop?

Lucy   I dunno, Mum. You choose.

Carol   No, let's do it together. Our passion project, just the two of us.

Silence. **Lucy** *carries on.*

Carol   I can take over that if you want?

Lucy   No, it's fine. I can do it.

Carol   Look what I've got here, *le beret pour tu* and *le beret pour* Carol.

Lucy   I'll put it on when I'm done.

Carol   Just leave that! Come on, we can't be late for Jean-Paul Pierre.

Lucy   I'm sure he won't mind.

Carol   I just want to make sure you're okay.

Lucy   I'm fine, Mum.

Carol   If you say so.

Lucy   Why don't you believe me?

Carol   Because I feel like we haven't really spent much time together.

Lucy   Funny that, because I was just thinking, I haven't seen anyone but you since the accident.

Carol   What about Aleesha?

Lucy   Don't want to talk about her!

Carol   Oh, like that is it?

Lucy   Like what?

Carol   I thought she would have been round to see you since the accident.

Lucy   Mum, it's none of your business.

Carol   It is my business! Call her a friend!

Lucy   Mum! Please! Leave me alone. You don't need to have eyes on me all the time.

Carol   I do if I don't want to spend all my time charging to and from the hospital!

Lucy   Anyone can have an accident! You can't just stop everything. Delete your entire social calendar to keep me safe. We'll go mad.

Carol   I am mad. I'm fucking furious. The minute my back's turned you're exercising your independence in A&E, via some seedy gin palace.

Lucy   Once, Mum, once!

Carol   So you keep saying, but it was one time too many for me. I can't take the stress of it, Lucy.

Lucy   Well, how do you think I feel being under twenty-four-hour surveillance?

Carol   Oh, now you're just exaggerating.

Lucy   I'm not, Mum!

Carol   I am simply trying my best to keep you safe!

Lucy   Mum! I am twenty-four. You were pregnant at my age!

Carol   Don't change the subject.

Lucy   You are suffocating me. I can't stand it!

Carol   For God's sake, Lucy, all I am trying to do is my best for you, and all you can do is scream at me. It's unacceptable. And it's not fair. Yes, I look after you. Who else is going to do it if I don't? There's hardly a queue forming of people willing to give a hand is there?

Pause.

And I want you to thrive, God, I want you to thrive. Do you know, the day you were born they told me you might die! Do you know what that did to me, Luce? What that does to a mother? It's not something you just 'get over' and then get on with, going about your business, like it's just another day in anywhere'sville. So, yes, I am protective of you. And yes, I am prepared to do whatever it takes to help me protect you. Tell me what mother wouldn't do the same if they were in my shoes.

Silence. **Lucy** *looks* **Carol** *in the eye, very deliberately turns on her wheelchair.* **Lucy** *doesn't look back.*

Carol   Lucy, where are you going?! Lucy!

The slam of the front door.

Scene Seven

Phone call

Lucy   Pick up, David . . .

Lucy *is in the back of a taxi.* **David***'s phone rings. Looks at it, eventually picks up.*

David   Hello.

Lucy   Are we going for a drink or what?

David   Is this a pocket dial?

Lucy   No, first round's on me.

David   Sorry . . . Me and my flatmates are heading to a gig.

Lucy   Which band?

David *says nothing.*

Lucy   Are you still there?

David   Spoon /

Lucy   You sure you got the energy for that.

She laughs. **David** *does not.*

Lucy   Look, if you change your mind you know where I'll be. Like I said, I'm buying. Don't keep me waiting.

Pause.

He puts the phone down.

Scene Eight

Bar

Lucy *is at a table alone. A bottle of wine and two glasses wait. She checks her phone. Nothing. Puts it face down on the table. Looks at it. Pushes it across the table as slowly as she can at arm's length. She looks at it. Suddenly it rings, she snatches it back. She can see it is her mum calling, she hangs up. Goes back to scrolling her messages.* **David** *enters, sees* **Lucy** *and goes over to her.*

Lucy   Hey. Glad you decided not to leave me hanging.

David   Sure you're not about to be joined by the cast of 'Me, My Friends, and my Entire Extended Family'? I know how much you like a surprise when you're entertaining.

Lucy   You turning up is enough of a surprise for me right now. What about your gig? Your flatmates?

David   I lied.

Lucy   Oh.

David   It isn't nice to be lied to, is it?

Lucy (*realises there is no gig*)   No.

Pause.

David   Why didn't you tell me that you lived with your mum?

Lucy   Oh because that's such an attraction isn't it?

David   I'd have been okay with it.

Lucy   Fuck off.

Pause.

David   Look, I'm sorry I flew off the handle. I just needed you to be straight with me.

Lucy   We both did shitty things.

Pause.

David   Is that why you called me? Clear your conscience?

Lucy   One of the reasons.

David   So, the others?

Lucy   You're the one doing a PhD, so come on mastermind, you tell me.

David   All right. So you've ordered wine, which I know you don't really like, but you know I do. Which is a nice gesture, shows you pay attention, you care and you're trying to win me over.

Lucy   Go on.

David   Which means you must think I'm worth winning over . . . and when I came in and saw you sitting there, I'm not going to lie, I'm appreciating the effort you've made.

Lucy   Not bad. But what effort are you going to make? You ran out on me remember?

David   Fair point. So let's drop the pretence and let me at least get you the drink of your desires.

Lucy   Why thank you. Your observation and gesture is much appreciated.

David *nods and* **Lucy** *nods him back.*

Lucy   But it's a bit early for cocktails, and let's not waste this, unless you were planning on sinking it all on your own.

David   No, I'm happy to share, sharing's good.

Lucy *fills the two glasses and then proposes a toast.*

Lucy   To us.

David   There's an 'us'?

Lucy *just looks at* **David***, in that way.*

David   Ok, to 'us'.

They drink. **Lucy***'s hand trembles and she spills some of her wine.*

Lucy   Fuck –

David *helps her mop it up.*

David   Shall I ask for a straw?

Lucy   I checked, the only ones they have are those small ones that fall into your glass. I questioned them about it and the man looked at me like I'd shouted 'Screw the Turtles'.

David   Shitemare.

Lucy   Hashtag DisabledExtinction.

David   Hashtag SurvivalOfTheFittest.

Lucy   Hashtag DavidIsOnFire.

David   Hashtag CoolMeDown.

Silence.

Lucy   Hashtag HappyHour Winky Face?

They snog.

David   Sex on the Beach?

Lucy   Go on then.

Scene Nine

Projection montage.

Text messages in screen reader voice.

Friday 23:01

David   *'Hope you got home safely and avoided all the kerbs.
crying/laughing face Too soon?'*

Lucy   *'Ha! Mum was furious! #CottonWoolMonster'*

David   *'She'll be fine. Once she meets me.'*

Lucy   *'Cock blocked by #CottonWoolMonster #SmellyFlatmates'*

Saturday 11:28

David   *'Can u come out and play today? I'm only 10 mins away.
winky face emoji'*

Lucy   *'Mum's on her way back from getting her booster, soz.
crying face emoji'*

Monday 21:07

David   *'Evening babe, asking for a friend, is it legal to have sex in
a public toilet?'*

Lucy   *'Googling . . . tell your 'friend' *crying/laughing face
emoji* outlawed under section 73 of the Sexual Offences Act 2003
. . .'*

David   *'Aww, my friend will be very disappointed. *smirky face
emoji*'*

Thursday 20:30

Lucy   *'Mum's having an early night . . . fancy a visitor?'*

David   *'Aargh I wish, Akshad's here. *facepalm emoji*'*

Saturday 10:32

Lucy   *'Morning, lover boy. I've got three words for you.'*

David   *'Omg, caught the feels?'*

Lucy   *'Shuttup! *facepalm emoji* Fuck me now.'*

David   *'*Aubergine emoji* Where?'*

Lucy   *'*Fire emoji* Here. Mum's gone shopping.'*

Lucy   *'David, the clock's ticking and my arse is getting cold!'*

Lucy   *'David??'*

David   *'On my way! I've had an idea!'*

Scene Ten

The Proposal

Lucy *and* **David** *in* **Lucy**'s *house.*

Lucy   A caravan?!

David   Yeah. It's my aunt and uncle's. They've said we can use it. It's free next weekend!

Lucy   That's your idea?!

David   Yes.

Lucy   I thought maybe you were dressing up, or stopping off at the sex shop for a few goodies.

David   I think we need our own space where we're alone for a bit. Just you and me.

Lucy   We're alone now, I wanna fuck now?

David   Your Mum could be back any minute.

Lucy   Come on!

David   No. I hate all this sneaking around like a loved-up teenager. I'm doing this for us. This is the chance for us to do what we want, when we want, as often as we want.

Lucy   Promises, promises.

David   Come on, Luce. Think about it.

Lucy   This better not be some pokey run-down shack with a Portaloo.

David   Hello. Think big, Lucy. The caravan is huge, it's got a flat-screen TV and a king-size bed.

Lucy   Ok, but what about care?

David   I'm suggesting this because I care.

Lucy   Funny . . . but seriously, who's going to be my p.a., because I'm not going on a weekend shag-fest with my mum in tow, nor am I willing to let some random stranger into the inner sanctum of my private life.

David   I'm not some random.

Lucy   David!

David   Well, I'm not exactly a stranger.

Lucy   You?

David   At your service.

Lucy   Oh for fucksake / you are joking aren't you?

David   I help you now don't I? I pass you stuff.

Lucy   Pass me stuff? I can't believe . . . who are you?

David   We can come up with a routine.

Lucy   I don't want to come up with a routine with you, David.

David   Why not?

Lucy   Because you're not my carer and to cross that line is just fucking weird.

David   Are you calling me a weirdo?

Lucy   No, but what you're proposing is . . . is not what I'm looking for in my lover. That's all.

Pause. (It's awkward. Eventually **Lucy** *moves towards* **David** *to appease him.)*

Lucy   And I really, really, really want you.

David   I know, but not like this . . .

Lucy   It's a lovely idea but being with me isn't as easy as you obviously think it is.

David   Don't say that. There must be a way.

Lucy   Well, I don't see one.

David   We'll think of something.

Lucy   Ok. You'd better go now. Mum'll be back with the shopping any minute, and I'd hate for her to get the wrong idea.

David   I've got three words for you . . . We won't fail.

David *goes.*

Scene Eleven

Lucy withdraws

Lucy *is lying down on her bed scrolling through her phone. We hear videos.* **Carol** *finishes putting newly ironed clothes in* **Lucy***'s wardrobe.*

Carol   Do you want to sit up then and I'll wash you?

Lucy   Hold on, let me watch this.

Carol   I don't understand how you can watch different people do the same dances over and over. It's beyond me.

Lucy   It's because you're old.

Carol   Charming. (*She tears the covers off* **Lucy**.) C'mon, attack the day.

Lucy   Urgh. (*She turns away.*) Nah, not yet.

Carol   No, come on. I've got a 'to do' list as long as a tapeworm today, I can't be hanging around waiting for you to agree to get ready when the mood takes you.

Lucy   I don't mind waiting if that's easier for you.

Carol   Ooh, like butter wouldn't melt. (*Pause,* **Lucy** *retreats to her phone.*) You working today?

Lucy   No.

Carol   OK, suspect you'll be off out?

Lucy   Dunno . . . *Netflix* probably.

Carol   Do you want to see if Aleesha is free?

Lucy   She's probably out with Luke.

Carol   Well, are you /

Lucy   Bloody hell, Mum, what's with the twenty questions?!

Carol   I have to ask don't I? You don't seem to want to get out of bed. Is it something I've done?

Lucy *exhales.*

Lucy   Mum, I've got something to tell you, but you have to promise not to get mad or panic or anything.

Carol *sits down on the bed. Pause.*

Carol   Well, go on then, Lucy love, what is it?

Lucy   You have to promise.

Carol   All right, all right I promise, just spit it out! Lord above, the suspense! My chest is so tight, I'll have to loosen my bra.

Lucy   Mum, I've been seeing someone

She expects a response. Nothing.

Mum, did you hear me? I have been going out with someone. His name is David.

Carol   Luce, that's great. I thought you were going to tell me something bad.

Lucy   You aren't mad?

Carol   Lucy, I sometimes wonder who you think I am. I wasn't born yesterday. It was obvious those lovely flowers at the hospital weren't from Aleesha, if only – a lentil burger's got more taste than that girl. Then Toni said you showed up with a handsome young man at her Zoom party, only a shame he didn't have the good manners to stop and say hello to his hostess. So, this really isn't a surprise, darling.

Lucy   Yeah, but, Mum, I met him on a dating app.

Carol   Ok.

Lucy   I know you hate those.

Carol   Yes, they are not my favourite, but /

Lucy   And he wants me to go away with him.

Carol   What? Where? When?

Lucy   A caravan in Minehead. Imagine?

Carol   Minehead is nice isn't it?

Lucy   Who are you and what have you done with my mother?

Carol   I'm tired of you feeling sorry for yourself.

Lucy   I'm not feeling sorry for myself.

Carol   Then get up, get washed and tell this David to prepare his caravan of love.

Lucy   That's the point, I can't do any of those things on my own can I?

Carol   Why are you doing it on your own? Hello! (*She points to herself.*)

Lucy   Mum, no, it's a weekend away . . . and . . .

Carol   Ok, right, I hear that, Lucy. But who's going to do your care?

Lucy   The only person I can think of is Aleesha.

Carol   No, not for me, thank you!

Lucy   I know I wasn't for one minute suggesting she was the answer.

Carol   I'll never forget the sight of her on CCTV hurtling down the high street in those shopping trolleys. How she kept her balance, legs astride two trolleys travelling at over fifteen miles an hour, I'll never know.

Lucy   It was her tribute to Lady Godiva.

Carol   Well, she's certainly gone down in history, with a suspended sentence and a lifetime ban from Asda.

Lucy   As I said, I'd already ruled out Aleesha.

Carol   You need someone who's going to take it seriously. Maybe it is time to try one of those agencies. Lots of people use them, Luce. They are professionals. We could finance it with your PIP.

Lucy   No. Not a stranger. Not yet. It's too soon, I'd be too nervous all of the time.

Carol   Okay . . .

Lucy   See, it's easier if I don't go.

Carol   Eureka! I've got it, how about Toni?

Lucy   What?

Carol   She's got experience of caring. She was wonderful with her Christine, right to the end.

Lucy   That was different.

Carol   How? They were partners, no different from you and me really.

Lucy   She's still grieving.

Carol   Then what better than an unexpected change of scenery.

Lucy   I don't know, Mum. Do you think she would?

Carol   Only one way to find out.

Lucy   Yeah, I suppose.

Carol   I'm helping her in the garden later, you can join us if you like, and just bring it up into conversation entirely naturally . . .

Lucy   Me asking her, but / I

Carol   Yes, Lucy, you. That's what people do when they want something.

Lucy   But what should I say? How should I approach her?

Carol   Well a clean pair of knickers'd be start / don't alienate your target

Lucy   Oi!

Carol   Then take a deep breath, open your mouth and engage your brain. Works wonders every time. I've never known you to be lost for words.

Lucy   Thanks, Mum.

They hug, but **Carol** *turns away as if* **Lucy** *smells. They laugh.* **Lucy** *offers her a hand to be helped up.*

Scene Twelve

Chat with Toni

The faint sound of a garden strimmer. **Lucy** *has an almost full black bin liner by the side of her chair.* **Toni**, *wearing gardening gear, holds branches and foliage, and whistles while she works.*

Toni   Here, shug, hold this bag.

Lucy *holds the bag. She's feeling a bit awkward.*

Lucy   Toni, would you say you're an outdoorsy person?

Toni   The hay fever makes it difficult . . .

Lucy   Would you say you liked the outside a little or a lot?

Toni   Enough to get my Bronze DofE.

Lucy   Toni . . . I need to ask you a question, it's a bit of a biggie.

Toni   Oh, ok.

Lucy   I've been asked if I'd like to go on holiday in a couple of weeks and I'd need someone to help . . . provide personal care . . . and we thought . . . I thought . . . maybe . . . you could be my personal assistant.

Toni   Me?

Lucy   Sorry. I should never have . . . it was stupid of me. Shall we go back in now, before / it starts getting –

Toni   No, no. It's fine. It wasn't stupid at all. You have to ask. I'm just surprised you thought of me that's all.

Lucy   Well, we all saw how well you looked after Christine, you did everything for her.

Toni   Yeah but Christine was my . . . till death do us . . . and all that.

Lucy   Yeah, of course, makes sense.

Pause.

Toni   What sort of thing would you need?

Lucy   Washing, dressing that type of thing. I need someone who I can really trust.

Toni   Ah, well, that's sweet . . .

Lucy   I'd pay you.

Toni   Hey now, I'll be having none of that.

Lucy   I'd have to pay you, Toni. It'd be your job. I couldn't do it otherwise. It wouldn't feel right. It's ok, I get allowance for care support.

Toni   Oh, ok, duck, I get it. If you really think I can help then I don't see why not.

Lucy   Toni, that's brilliant. You're a lifesaver.

Toni   I don't know about that.

Lucy   I'm going with David.

Toni   David, from the party?

Lucy   Yeah, we've been dating.

Toni   Good for you!

Lucy   And his family have got a caravan in Somerset.

Toni   Oh, I see like that is it.

Lucy   No, it's just /

Toni   Makes no odds to me, get it whilst you're young I say. You anna lived until you've tickled some tonsils under some tarpaulin.

Lucy   Toni!

Toni   When are we going? I can pop into town and pick up a few supplies from Ann Summers if you like. There's nothing beats going bareback in a bivouac.

Lucy   See, this is exactly why I knew you'd be great! We'd take the train down to Minehead on the Friday and stay until the Sunday /

Toni   Minehead? Isn't that a bit far? I'm a bit of a planner you see and I might need things I anna got. I'd need time too which you really haven't got.

Lucy   What would you need specifically? We can get it for you.

Toni   I inna a charity. Look as you say there's a lot to it and I think I've jumped the gun.

Lucy   We'd have a great weekend.

Toni   I've no doubt you would but the weekends inna any good for me really. I don't think I can do it.

Lucy   What? You seemed so /

Toni   It was my fault. Sorry, I got carried away for a minute. I wasn't thinking.

Lucy   But /

Toni   I just don't think its for me.

She gets up quickly.

Lucy   Can we talk?

Toni   My hay fever. It's gone to my eyes. I need to get a tissue.

She leaves with tears in her eyes.

Lucy   Toni!

Lucy   Arse! Well that went well, Lucy Lou. Not! Why can't life be simple? Arrgghhh! Aleesha gets to go to Lanzarote. I can't even get to Minehead!

She goes to text **David***:*

Lucy (*leaving voice note or voicing for text*)   '*Hey babe, hope work okay. Toni said no. Back to square one. *sad face emoji*'*

Toni *enters with a tissue*

Toni   Okay shug, I'll do it.

Lucy   Really?

Toni   Yes. I'd love to go with you both.

Lucy   Toni, that's great. Thank you.

Toni   Minehead you see, it's where my Christine proposed to me.

Lucy   Sorry Toni, I didn't realise.

Toni   No shug, you weren't to know. I had a word with myself and know Christine would want me to go. It'll be good for me. Ideally I'd need someone to let Scargill in at night mind, so if your Mum can do that.

Lucy   I'm sure she can.

Toni   Alright, we better start packing. And me and you, well we need to get all our ducks in a row, duck.

Scene Thirteen

Train station

Bing bong. Train announcements over the Tanoy. **David** *is eating a big bag of Doritos.* **Lucy** *is on her phone.*

Lucy (*on the phone*)   Did you . . . pack the sun cream? I've looked at the weather and it doesn't look too bad . . . No, I thought you did but then I thought maybe I was imagining it . . . Do you know what? I don't think I've been so chill. No, Mum, I'm really fine. So fine . . . I'll call you later? . . . I mean, I might not need you, but if I do . . . Right. I'm going, I'm going . . . love you, bye.

She puts the phone down.

David   You knew she packed the sun cream didn't you?

Lucy   You can never be too sure.

David   But you can because you checked the list three times.

Lucy   I was just checking she's alright –

David   She's only been gone twenty minutes. Please believe me, she will be fine.

Lucy *checks her watch.*

Lucy   Where's Toni?

David   She's only five minutes late –

Lucy   That's not the point, David. We said quarter to by the big Costa. Try again.

David   I just did. Maybe she's stuck in traffic.

Lucy   Try again /

David   If she's driving.

Lucy   David!

David *dials his phone.*

David (*on the phone*)   Hi, Toni, it's David. We're by the big Costa and we're just wondering where you are. Can you give me a ring when you get this please?

He puts the phone down.

Lucy   It's completely ridiculous /

David   We've still got a while yet. Hey, let's send your mum a selfie.

Lucy   If you're doing a selfie you'll need this.

She pretends to be getting something out of her bag, and then just gives **David** *the finger.*

David   Oh, middle finger, classy. Come on then let's find the access lounge, and make our presence known.

Lucy   This is where we agreed to meet.

David   If we walk up we might bump into her. (*He starts to move ahead slightly.*) C'mon, Lucy.

Toni *enters whistling.*

Lucy   Toni, where have you been? Quarter to we said.

David   Well, we're all here now /

Toni *takes the rucksack off her back, puts it on the floor and begins to unzip various compartments.*

Toni   Sorry! Charger conked, then turns out their card machine had done the same.

Lucy   It's really not good enough, anything could have happened. If this is how it's started I dread to think how the rest of the holiday is going to turn out.

Toni *digs through rucksack.*

Toni   I was getting batteries as it happens. Do you know, it's like being a flying picket again.

Lucy   A flying what? We're getting a train, Toni. What do you need batteries for?

Toni   Like when I was a union organiser back in the early eighties. Taking industrial action at a moment's notice, standing shoulder to shoulder on the picket lines. (*Pulls out three walkie-talkies.*) Ah, here are the bleeders! Right at the bottom. Here you go. (*Handing them out for* **David** *and* **Lucy**.) I got one for each of us.

David   Ahh, walkie-talkies, ace!

Toni   Number one rule is, you've always got to stay in touch. (*She messes with her set.*) Channel six I think I'm on.

David   These are good aren't they, Luce?

Lucy   If you're fourteen and it's 1972, perhaps?

Toni   Give it a go, go on! (*Through the radio.*) Lucy in the sky with diamonds, do you read? Over.

Lucy   What?

Toni   I've given us names so it's proper. You can call me Head Shoulders Knees and Tone. Over.

Lucy *clicks her radio on.*

David   Once in Royal David's City receiving, over!

Toni   Hey, did you come up with that all by yourself? Over.

David   I think these are just what we need. Smashing, aren't they, Lucy?

Pause.

Lucy   I suppose they might come in useful. Over?

Toni   High praise indeed.

Lucy   Sorry, I didn't mean to fly off the handle. I just want everything to be okay, y'know.

Toni   Of course you do, it being your first time /

Lucy   Toni! Not so loud . . . and no it's not as it goes.

Toni   I was talking about you being away from home without your mum.

Lucy   Oh. Right. Yes. Thank you, Toni. Very thoughtful.

Toni   Right, off to the access lounge. Wagons roll!

David   Oh God, I bet she claps when the plane lands.

Scene Fourteen

Need a wee

Lucy *is sat in her chair under a table on a train with a crossword in front of her.* **David** *is out of his chair opposite her.* **Toni** *is a few rows behind them, doing a cross-stitch. There's bundles of wool on her table.*

Lucy   Fourteen across. Growth. Eleven letters. Something E. Something M. Something N. Something T.I.O.N.

David   I'm shit at crosswords, plus I can't focus when I'm malnourished.

Lucy   Honestly, you're like a twelve-year-old. (*Of the crossword.*) Eleven down. US nineties tennis ace. Six letters. Agassi. Yes!

David   Not to mention parched!

Lucy   Come on, it is almost finished, if you put your mind to it. (*Over radio.*) Toni, would you mind coming up here, please?

Toni (*comes up through the aisle*)   What can I do for you?

Lucy   Toni, are you sure you wouldn't like to come and sit with us?

Toni   Honestly, duck, I am fine back there.

Lucy (*to* **Toni**)   What are you cross-stitching? (*Reading from it.*) Minehead Chippy.

Toni   I like to do a little scene wherever I go somewhere, keeps me active y'know.

Lucy   How good is that, David?? Look at the little bench.

David   Yes, good . . .

Toni   Let me know if you need anything else. (*She goes to sit.*)

David   Now leave her in peace to finish it, Luce.

Lucy (*to* **David**)   I don't want her to be alone. (*To* **Toni** *over the radio.*) There is a seat right here if you change your mind.

Toni (*to* **Lucy** *over the radio*)   No, thanks, number one rule of the branch – never mix business and pleasure. You kids just enjoy yourselves.

David (*gently takes the radio off of her*)   Lucy, I can't wait any longer!

He locks eyes with her as if this is the beginning of him trying to create the perfect romantic holiday for them. From a bag beneath the table, he reaches a gingham cloth and spreads it across the table.

Hold on.

He puts a small LED candle in the centre of the table.

Ta da!

She puts down the crossword and starts to play along. He takes out some cocktail sausages.

Lucy   I was hoping for salami, but I guess those will do.

He pulls out a can of Pringles.

Lucy   'Once you pop, you can't stop.'

He pulls out some some cheese and crackers and places them on the table. She starts to make a quip and he places his finger over her lips to stop her, but in a flirty way.

He pulls out a container with a lid and places it on the table.

David   And now for the beautiful woman fixing my gaze . . .

He places an empty water bottle next to the candle and out of his coat pocket he retrieves a single yellow daffodil.

Ta da!

Lucy   Where did you get that from?

David   I've got my contacts in the municipality.

Lucy   So you nicked it from the park.

David   The universe helps those who help themselves.

He whips off the lid to reveal chocolate-covered strawberries.

Now help yourself to some of these . . . (*They both start to eat.*)

Lucy   David, thank you. All this, it's special.

David   Because you're special.

Lucy   So are you. (*After a short while a smirk emerges on* **Lucy**'s *face.*)

David   What?

Lucy   You're not the only one with a surprise.

David   Oh yeah?

Lucy   Yeah, but you're going to have to wait once we've arrived.

David   Ok.

Lucy   Yeah, what do you say to christening the bed, soon as we get there, Mr Loverman? Seeing as you've so perfectly set the mood.

David   I like surprises and I like your style.

Lucy   I promise you'll like what I've got in store, once we're behind closed doors.

David   Well until then . . .

He puts the two cups in front of him on the table.

(*In a mock French accent.*) . . . the piece you will not be able to resist . . .

He pulls something from the bag.

I bring you, Sex on the Beach . . . in cans! . . . Tantric tins, if you will!

He goes to pour for **Lucy**. *She stops him.*

Lucy   None for me thanks.

David   Come on, I've been keeping it on ice for long enough / now it's time to get . . .

Lucy   No, honestly. I don't want a drink yet, I can't . . .

David   What?

Pause.

Lucy   I need to pee.

David   Didn't you go before we left?

Lucy   Yeah, alright, Mum. (*Beat.*) It's alright. I'll wait until we get there.

David   You can't do that can you?

Lucy   We've not got long.

David   Yeah, we have. An hour to be exact. You're going to have to go.

Lucy   No. I don't like to wee on trains. The toilets are disgusting.

David   Lucy, come on, it's really not a good idea to hold it in for so long, you could do real damage to yourself.

Lucy   Stop talking about it. I'm fine.

David   You're clearly not. You've got Toni here, it's what she's for. I'm just thinking of you, and the mood . . .

Lucy   Ok.

David *hands* **Lucy** *the walkie-talkie. She presses the button on the radio.*

Lucy   Heads, toes, knees and shoulders or whatever . . . look, Toni . . . can you just come and see me, please, out, I mean over?

Toni   Hello, Lucy in the Sky with Diamonds, do you copy? Over.

Lucy   Yes, knees I copy, I big time copy. I need to use the toilet. So can you put this silly toy down and come over here now? Over. Please.

Toni   Message understood, Lucy in the Sky with Diamonds. Over and out.

She comes over to **Lucy** *and* **David**.

Toni   I'll go and do a recce, duck. Be right back.

She leaves.

David   I'll get the cocktails ready.

Lucy   No, thanks.

Toni *enters.*

Toni   Report from the frontline. Good news, there is an accessible toilet. The rest of the news is all bad. Let's say, you'll not be the first one to use those facilities, of which there is plenty of trace evidence, complete with toxic aroma and the door is broken . . .

David   Fuckinell –

Lucy   It's fine. I'll wait.

David   Can we have a word with someone? A manager or something.

Toni   I anna seen anyone on here.

Lucy   I don't want to make a fuss –

Toni   Well, you bleeding well should. It dunna matter about anyone else.

Pause.

Oh lovey, I know it inna ideal but you shouldn't have to hold yourself. Why don't we give it a go? Put your face mask on and I can hold the door.

David   We'll stand outside and guard it if we have to. I'm not having you feeling shit on the first day of your holiday, Lucy. Sorry wrong choice of words, but I've got your back.

Lucy (*to* **David**)   No. No. No. You stay here. Toni, come with me.

They go to the toilet, leaving **David**. *Pause. Almost a peaceful silence, when suddenly the train jolts, throwing* **David** *forward in his seat. From off we hear* **Lucy** *shriek and shout 'fuck' multiple times.*

Toni *enters.*

David   Where's Lucy, what's going on?

Toni   There's been a spillage. She wants to complete the journey in there.

David   What? She can't. She can't occupy the toilets for another hour, with you guarding the door, besides she'll be overcome by the fumes.

Toni   It's just a bit awkward, David, she's not really rockin' the beach-ready look right now. If you get me.

David   Yeah, I get you.

He grabs the gingham tablecloth and exits to the toilet. Moments later he returns with **Lucy** *who has the tablecloth wrapped around her legs.*

Lucy   I smell and people will stare.

David   So let them. This is our time and nothing's gonna burst our bubble. Besides, you look hot in a gingham tablecloth. Now, let's drink. To us christening that bed!

He pours the cocktails and they drink.

Scene Fifteen

Caravan

David *and* **Lucy** *are in the middle of the caravan.*

David   Here she is. Our own little slice of paradise.

Lucy   Smaller than it looks in the picture.

David   Sometimes happens on photos though doesn't it, scale and whatnot? I'll give you the grand tour in a bit. (*To off.*) Let me give you a hand with those bags, Toni.

Toni *enters dragging luggage behind her.*

Toni (*breathless*)   No you're all right, just a bit out of practice. I could carry twice this load when I did my Duke of Edinburgh. Won't take me long to get back up to speed. Though right now I think I need a brew and a bit of a sit down.

David   Brilliant! Aunty June said there was some milk in the fridge.

Lucy   Erm, do you . . . do you want to go get your caravan set up, Toni? We can manage here.

Toni   Let me at least make you a cuppa tea? (**Toni** *goes over to the kitchen and starts making tea*.) Want one, David?

Lucy   I haven't come here to drink tea, Toni.

David   Yeah, I think I really need to get horizontal after that long journey.

Toni (*getting the hint*)   Actually, it's not really tea I'm after right now. Think I'm just going to go do the same, that is lie down for a bit, on my own, in my quarters.

She leaves.

David   You have to see the bedrooms. A-mazing there's lava lamps.

Lucy   Oh, great.

David   Are you alright?

Lucy   Yeah, I'm fine. Just a bit stuffy isn't it?

David   I can solve that problem.

Lucy   Are they handprints?

David   Er, dunno. I think they're just factory prints, from Ikea, nothing special.

Lucy   I'm not talking about the pictures, I mean there, on the window.

David   Oh, it's just the way the light catches it at this time of day I reckon.

Lucy   They're definitely handprints.

David   And?

Pause.

Lucy, what's the matter?

Lucy   Nothing . . . it's fine. Everything's fine.

David   Fine? Really?

Lucy   I just. I was expecting something with a bit more room. You know, a bit more pizazz.

David   We've been here five minutes. You haven't even done the grand tour yet.

Lucy   For fuck's sake. There's a bit of dried jam on this table, cobwebs under the units.

Toni   We can clean up. We've got, Toni.

Lucy   We? She's not our valet! Besides, no one should have to spend the first hours of their holiday cleaning.

David   Well, excuse me, I'm sorry, the caravan me and my family have spent the last fifteen years holidaying in, up to our necks in blissful ignorance and muck, isn't up to your standards!

Lucy   I don't have *standards,* but this is below the tidemark of basic cleanliness!

David   What? This is a five-berth luxury caravan. It's vintage.

Lucy   A vintage shithole!

David   Fucking what?

Lucy   You heard!

Silence.

David   Right, well I am going to go get some milk, and some air . . . this isn't the start to our holiday either of us had in mind. I won't be long and when I get back we can . . . well . . . deep breaths and all that. I'll come back in and start again.

He leaves. A moment passes.

Lucy   Shit, shit, shithole!

Scene Sixteen

Ready

Lucy *is sat in her chair looking glam with cleavage.* **Toni** *helps her apply lipstick.*

Toni   Right, keep still.

Toni *applies to* **Lucy.**

Toni   Come on, duck, it's not that bad.

Lucy *just gives* **Toni** *a look.*

Toni   Ok, so it's not the Hilton, but he never said it was, and really you're not here to admire the scenery.

Lucy   I know.

Toni   Gotta keep your eye on the prize, young lady.

Lucy   You're right, and I know he's really trying. I'm just so jumpy.

Toni   Perfectly nautral, it's to be expected.

Lucy   Really?

Toni   Course and it's easily sorted – draw those curtains, some soft lighting and some soulful tunes and you'll both soon realise you've got everything you need once you're in each other's arms.

Lucy   You make it sound so simple.

Toni   That's because it is. So let's get you freshened up and ready for when the wanderer returns. You want to make the most of every minute don't you? There we go.

Lucy *grabs her compact mirror, pouts.*

Lucy   How do I look?

Toni   Boy's gonna have a heart attack when he walks in. You look magic, love, I'm so excited for you!

Lucy   Ooh, perfume!

Toni   Calvin – get your tackle out of my face – Klein, now that is classy. Much more of this, girl, and I'm gonna have to be jumping on one of them dating apps meself.

Lucy   Now the music.

Toni *picks up* **Lucy***'s phone.*

Toni   Any song?

Lucy   The Paolo Nutini one please.

Toni *clicks the phone accordingly. 'Last Request' by Paolo Nutini plays.*

Lucy   What way do you reckon? Facing the door or . . .

Toni   I don't know, love.

Lucy   Or maybe I should face away from him, it's more mysterious that way, don't you think?

Toni   I think you should do what's comfortable for you.

Lucy   Is he milking this cow or what? Why are men?

Toni   Can't help you in that department I'm afraid, love, not my flavour.

Lucy   You're lucky.

Toni   Are you joking? Women are just as much of a jigsaw.

She laughs.

Pause.

Lucy   I'm nervous.

Toni   Told you. it's normal to be nervous, duck. Enjoy it.

Lucy   Toni.

Toni   Why are you being so coy about it?! Nothing about sex is weird. Martini, that's my mantra. Their advertising slogan was anytime, anywhere.

Lucy   Toni, you dark horse.

Toni   You've no idea. Adopt the way of the Martini, my girl, and there's no looking back. One of my finest hours, 1985, a Support the Miners Rally in Newcastle-under-Lyme, me and my new best friend, butt naked under the stage. While the speakers above us whipped the crowd up into a frenzy, we had our own frenzy that needed whipping.

Lucy   Bloody hell.

Toni   Yeah. Turns out her dad was the local head of the sodding National Coal Board. I certainly took one for the team that day, I can tell you. Right, all ready to go?

Lucy   Yes!

Toni   Have you got everything before I get out of your hair?

Lucy   Yes, I'm fine I think.

Toni   Great, well. I'll be over at mine with a book and some earplugs – have fun.

Toni *leaves.* **Lucy** *waits, music is heard from a speaker. She waits.*

A text from **Lucy** *to* **David***: 'Come home, I've got a surprise. *Wink face*.'*

Lights fade.

Scene Seventeen

Not quite

We hear **David***'s voice singing 'Whole Again' by Atomic Kitten on karaoke.*

In the club. The music is louder. **Lucy** *finds* **David** *on the stage.*

Lucy   David! David!

Still singing.

David, come down from there.

David   Oh, look everyone, it's Lucy. Get the feather dusters and the Mr Sheen out. Whey! We've put a whole new spin on the meaning of a dirty weekend.

Lucy   Can you get down please?

David   I'm having far too much fun.

Lucy   David!

He wheels over to her. He carries a drink. They sit down by the bar.

Silence.

Lucy   So where's the milk?

David   I bought some, but as soon as I got it on site, it turned sour.

Lucy   So what are you doing here, this wasn't the plan?

David   I would've invited you but I didn't think you'd want to be seen in a dive like this.

Lucy   Why didn't you answer my calls? I've even had to use the fucking walkie-talkie.

David   This? There's probably more life under our bed than there is in these batteries.

He shows her the walkie-talkie with no back and one battery. He flicks the remaining one across the room.

Lucy   Dickhead.

David   Snobhead.

Lucy   That's not even a . . . I waited for you. I was ready for you, and I thought you felt the same.

David   When did you start thinking about my feelings?

Lucy   Look, the caravan wasn't exactly what I had in mind. I was just taken aback that's all.

David   Not so taken aback you couldn't stop for one second before sharing your worldly wisdom and making your judgement.

Lucy   David. I'm not judging you, or anyone. I just want it to be special.

David   Do you not think I want that to?

Lucy   I don't know. If you ghost me, how could I possibly know what you want?

David   Luce, you are the best thing that's happened to me . . . ever. I've never met anyone like you before, and I got scared I was getting it wrong, because . . .

Pause.

I'm really sorry.

Lucy   I'm sorry, I was nervous too. I'm glad I'm here with you.

David   Me too. You look so good in that dressing gown, even my wheels have gone stiff.

Scene Eighteen

Don't come a-knocking

A dark stage. The sound of wheelchairs bumping into furniture. Snogging. Lights up. Both in a state of undress. **David**'s *trousers down with boxers showing.* **Lucy**'s *top hanging off her shoulder.* **David** *tries to undo his shirt buttons but his fingers get stuck.*

Lucy   Do you want me to help –

David   No. It's fine.

Lucy   Sorry. Yeah.

David   Do you wanna get Toni? I can hold it /

Lucy   No, fuck it. We'll do it here.

David Are you sure?

Lucy Yes! C'mon.

David Just gotta put a johnny on.

Lucy If you just take my leg?

David Is that right?

Lucy Yes, that's it.

David If I just put my hands here . . .

Lucy Yeah, that's good.

David Let me just switch legs.

Pause.

Lucy Are you in?

David Yeah, I think so.

Silence. Panting. Quiet sex. It does not last long. A sigh.

Scene Nineteen

The Morning After

Bedroom. **David** *enters and finds* **Lucy** *in the kitchen making tea.*

Lucy Morning.

David Morning.

Lucy Tea?

David No. Thanks.

Lucy Toast?

David No, thanks.

Lucy Not hungry?

David No, I don't think so.

Lucy   No, me neither, actually.

Pause.

So /

David   What do you want to do / today?

Lucy   Last night –

David   Oh, yes right / last night

Lucy   Today?

Pause.

David   I thought we could have an adventure.

Lucy   Right. Nice.

David   Yes, stunning views.

Lucy   Lovely.

David   And easy pathways.

Lucy   Perfect.

David   Yeah, they've really thought about it, really made an effort. Because they care. They really care.

Lucy   I know they care, it's clear they care. So it's only right we show our appreciation and make an effort isn't it?

David   Great, I'm all for making an effort.

Lucy   I know.

David   Because that's how you get better isn't it? The harder you try, the better things get, that's what I've always found. The second time is better than the first, the third better than the second and –

Lucy   Ok, David, I get it.

David   Brilliant, I knew you would . . .

He goes to kiss **Lucy***, she pulls back.*

David   . . . shit. It was shit wasn't it.

Lucy   David, let's just –

David   I'm sorry, I was just so –

Lucy   It's ok. But let's just go out and enjoy our surroundings, no pressure.

David   But I want it . . . I want you . . . it has to be –

Lucy   It doesn't have to be anything more than it is. Let's just be . . .

David   Be . . .?

Lucy   Organic.

David   Organic?

Lucy   Let's go out, like you said and let it be whatever it will be.

David   But I want –

Lucy   David, let's not force it. Let's just feel our way through the day.

David   Ok. (*Pause.*) I'm sorry –

Lucy   No apologies, let's just . . . be.

She exits.

Lucy (*from off*)   Well, come on, seize the day!

David   Shit, I think I've slept with Yoda.

He exits too.

Scene Twenty

Projection montage.

A series of images show the following:

Hoopla. **Lucy** *throws three discs, which land way off target.* **David** *laughs. It's his turn and the same thing happens.* **Lucy** *revels in his failure.*

Lucy *has a cuddly toy in the grabber machine. It hovers over the slot but breaks. They hit the machine; it doesn't come loose.* **David** *whacks the machine.* **Lucy** *is annoyed so she walks away.*

Rain. **David** *and* **Lucy** *are under a canopy. Miserable.*

David   Shall we try hoopla again? I think I've warmed up my wrists now.

Lucy   I'm not sitting in the pissing rain so you can have a dick-swinging contest with the bloke on the stall.

David   I swear he was fudging the game. (*Putting his hand outside to feel the rain.*) It's easing up now –

Lucy   It really isn't.

David   Well, at least it was fun while the rain held off.

Lucy   It really wasn't.

David   Ok Ms. I'm so happy I could cry. What do you want to do? –

Lucy   Anything that doesn't involve skidding, getting muddy tire marks on all your clothes and spending two hours under a hand dryer trying to re-establish your proper body temperature.

David   Shame, I just put us down for the mud wrestling tournament.

Lucy   You're out of luck, hombre, you'll have to find another tag partner.

David   Story of my life.

Pause.

I know just the thing to get your pulse racing.

Lucy   David, I thought we'd agreed /

David   I'm not talking about that. I'm talking about Laser Quest.

Lucy   Hashtag I've officially just hit my all-time low.

David   Come on, it's indoor, there's no mud, but there might be blood.

Lucy *turns away.*

Lucy   Shall we just go pack?

David   Chicken.

Lucy   Are you for real?

David   I just thought you were the kind of person who was up for laughs.

Lucy   It's hardly age appropriate.

David   Didn't know there was a certificate rating on fun. Or is it just that you're scared?

Lucy   Ok, Mr Gobshite. Laser Quest it is. And don't turn your back on me, that's all I'm saying.

Scene Twenty-One

Laser Quest

We join them mid-game laser tag. They've retreated behind a box. **David** *breathless. He inspects his gun.*

David   Why didn't you cover me?!

Lucy   I can't do much if you don't shoot.

David   I am shooting, it's my gun that's shit!

Lucy *pokes her head out the side of the box and shoots a couple of rounds.*

Lucy   Take that, you rug rats!

She goes to move but **David** *stops her.*

David   You can't move yet, we've got no game plan. They'll destroy us!

Lucy They're eight years old, David. I don't think we need a game plan against a bunch of over-achieving year threes.

David That's what they want you to think. They lull you into a false sense of security and render you useless leaving you in a constant state of respawn because they keep fucking shooting at you!

He gets shot from behind.

Ouch!

Lucy Do you not think you're taking this a bit *too* seriously?

David Serious. We're in a bloody war zone.

Lucy Yes, I know. It's great. Now, if you don't mind, I'm off to make some children cry, and then wet themselves.

She makes to leave, but **David** *grabs her and stops her in her tracks.*

David Listen! If we don't stick together there's a real possibility they'll overwhelm us and we may never see each other again.

Lucy *turns around and shoots him.*

David Ow! What the . . . What was that for?

Lucy I'm programmed to hunt emotionally immature and inarticulate men . . . and shoot on sight.

She shoots him again. **David** *flinches.*

David We're on the same team –

Lucy Yeah, well. I've gone rogue.

She shoots him again.

David Ow! Fuck . . . will you . . . /

Lucy Yep, still inarticulate.

She shoots him again.

David Fuck! Lucy I'm /

She shoots him again.

Ok, Ms. I was born with a silver duster up my arse! I warned you.

He shoots.

Lucy   Shit! Shit! You asshole! Eat this, you jerk, for making me traipse through the whole campsite in my dressing gown!

She shoots.

David   This is for lying about living with your mum!

He shoots.

Lucy   You're so pathetic. This is for thinking I could ever be impressed by a shithole like this!

She shoots.

David   This is for calling the family getaway a shithole!

He shoots.

Lucy   This is for cumming too quickly and not holding me afterwards!

She shoots. They've started to move closer.

David   This is for not being there when I woke up this morning because it actually made me really sad! I hate you so much!

He shoots. Closer still.

Lucy   I hate you more!

David   More?!

Lucy   More! This is for you coming to see me in hospital, when you didn't even know me. More?!

David   This is for you ringing me up out of the blue and inviting me out for a drink.

They kiss.

Is this organic enough for you?

Lucy   Yes, totally natural.

David   But the caravan is miles away.

Lucy   True, but the toilets here are really big and really clean.

David   The toilets?

Lucy   Here, yes.

David   Clean?

Lucy   Yes.

David   Clean enough for you?

Lucy   Yes, they're pristine and it's got a hoist. (*Pause.*) Is that your walkie-talkie or is it your little friend?

David *takes out the walkie-talkie.*

David   David to Toni, code red, repeat code red hot!

What if someone tries to get in?

Lucy   Radar key and a double lock.

As if by magic, **Toni** *appears.*

Toni   Alright. Just had a lovely stroll along the beach.

Lucy   Sounds good. I really need the loo, can you give us a hand?

Toni   Rightio, let's get you sorted shall we?

Transition into the toilet.

Lucy   There's a hoist here, shame not to use it.

Toni   I anna ever used it before but we'll give it a go, eh?

Lucy   I only need you to put me in the hoist.

Toni   Come on then, love.

Lucy *is put into the hoist.*

Lucy   You can go on, Toni. David can do the rest, can't you?

David   Yeah, we'll be fine.

Toni   Oh . . . right. Excellent, say no more, that's really excellent that is. I'll just wait out here shall I?

Toni *exits.*

David   Ready?

Lucy   Ready.

Scene Twenty-Two

Accessible Toilet

David *and* **Lucy** *have sex, with* **Lucy** *in the hoist. It is brilliant. Almost like a ballet.*

Scene Twenty-Three

Chips

Toni   I'd like to propose a toast. To freedom of expression!

David *and* **Lucy**   To freedom of expression!

They cheers.

Toni   I've had a smashing time.

Pause.

We did, didn't we? We did it.

Lucy *and* **David**   Yes, we did!

Lucy   Again.

David   And again.

Toni   All right, show-offs.

Lucy   To Laser Quest!

The toast and drink.

All   Laser Quest!

Scene Twenty-Four

Home

David *and* **Lucy** *are sat on the sofa.* **Lucy** *is on his laptop.* **David** *is looking through his phone.*

David   I booked the posh Italian place.

Lucy   Not everyday we celebrate you getting your doctorate.

David   And I really wanted to book something fancy under doctor.

Lucy   Can't wait to be under you later tonight, doctor!

David*'s phone goes;* **Toni** *on FaceTime.*

David   Look who it is!

He holds the phone up to him and **Lucy***.*

Lucy   Hey, Toni!

Toni   Hello, lovebirds!

Lucy   Did you see David in his cap and gown?

Toni   I did! Sat there and watched live with popcorn. You look really good in HD, y'know. (*Pause.*) Look at the pair of you, you're beaming.

David   Relieved it's over and done with.

Toni   I'd thought I'd keep this as a surprise for you both but I had my booster this afternoon. That's my vaccine passport bang up to date.

Lucy   That's great!

David   Does that mean we can book Magaluf?!

Toni   I've already ironed my bikini! Listen, I wunna keep you. Enjoy tonight and lots of love to all!

Lucy   Bye, Toni!

David   See you soon.

He puts the phone down. They kiss.

Ah, what a day!

They hug. Suddenly, a shriek of laughter is heard.

Carol   I'll be right back, Mark!

Carol *enters, her hair is ruffled. She freezes in the doorway.*

Lucy   Mum!

Carol   Luce, David. I didn't think you 'd be back yet. I thought I had a free yard tonight.

Lucy   A free yard?! Who are you?

Carol   Darling, don't be silly, you know perfectly well /

David   And what's up with you? You look like you've been dragged through a hedge backwards.

Carol   Well, it's windy out /

Lucy   And who the fuck is Mark?

Carol   Erm . . . no one . . . a friend . . . from spin . . . it finished early. Anyway, congratulations, David!

She quickly exits.

Lucy   A friend from spin?

David   Hashtag . . .

Lucy   . . . wheels on fire.

David *and* **Lucy** *kiss.*

They wheel off stage together without hitting any kerbs.

End.

CPSIA information can be obtained
at www.ICGtesting.com
Printed in the USA
LVHW042118290322
714724LV00015B/2253

9 781350 338975